PUBLISHED BY ROBERT CORBIN

VEGAN DIET: QUICK & EASY HIGH-PROTEIN VEGAN RECIPES

@ Mark Hicks

Published By Robert Corbin

@ **Mark Hicks**

Vegan diet: Quick & Easy High-protein

Vegan Recipes

All Right RESERVED

ISBN 978-87-94477-94-9

TABLE OF CONTENTS

Easy Carrot Slaw With Smoky Maple Tempeh Triangles.. 1

Bangkok Black Rice Salad 5

Lentil Salad In Olive Oil 8

Hemp Protein Granola Bars... 10

Quinoa With Acorn Squash 13

Mellow Lentil Soup... 16

Vegan Salad 18

Peppers Stuffed With Veggies... 21

Cranberry Chickpea Salad 23

Tofu Scramble 'Eggs' 25

Tempe Sweet Potato Scrambled 'Eggs'......................... 27

Chickpea Onion Omelet 29

Strawberry Muffins 31

Carrot Apple Muffins.. 33

Banana Muffins 36

Stuffed Portobello Mushrooms....................................... 37

Coconut Curry Noodles 41

Roasted Brussels Sprouts With Balsamic Glaze 45

Chickpea And Spinach Curry 48

Lentil Walnut Loaf 50

Teriyaki Tofu Stir-Fry 52

Traditional Miso Ramen With Silken Tofu 54

Red Curry Miso Ramen With Roasted Cauliflower 56

Peanut Miso Ramen With Spinach And Crispy Shallots . 58

Chocolate-Covered Strawberries 60

Banana Chocolate Chip Cookies 62

Berry Nice Cream 63

Peanut Noodle Salad 65

Broccoli Edam Me Salad 67

Arugula Green Beans Salad 69

Vegan Keto Chili 71

Eggplant Lasagna Rolls 74

Almond-Crusted Tofu Nuggets 76

Red Curry Quinoa Fried Rice 78

Alfredo Sauce 80

- Mac And Cheese 82
- Quinoa Salad With Creamy Balsamic Dressing 85
- Sprouted Mung Bean Salad 88
- Black & White Bean Quinoa Salad 90
- Lemony Blueberry Oatmeal 93
- Tomato Toast With Balsamic Drizzle 95
- Miso Maple Tofu Steaks 97
- Butternut Squash Slaw 99
- Thai Soup 101
- Zucchini Soup 103
- Butternut Squash With Mustard Vinaigrette 105
- Keto Vanilla Pancakes 107
- Keto-Friendly Vegan Cauliflower Hash Browns 109
- Simple Coconut Keto Vegan Pancakes 111
- Strawberry Applesauce Muffins 113
- Lemon Squares 115
- Quinoa Salad 117
- Jackfruit Tacos With Mango Salsa 121

Citrus Miso Ramen With Grilled Tempeh 127

Miso Ramen With Kimchi And Enoki Mushrooms 129

Pumpkin Miso Ramen With Sage-Infused Broth 131

Baked Cauliflower Wings 133

Mini Veggie Pizzas 135

Lentil And Veggie Patties 137

Black Bean Lentil Salad 139

Easy Carrot Slaw With Smoky Maple Tempeh Triangles

Ingredients:

- 1 Tbsp crushed raw walnuts
- 4 cups shredded carrots
- 1 small onion, diced
- 1 Tbsp curry powder
- 1/4 tsp turmeric powder for added turmeric power, optional
- 1/8 tsp black pepper
- 2 Tbsp tahini
- 1/4 cup fresh lemon juice
- sweet stuff: 1 - 1 1/2 Tbsp maple syrup + an optional handful or raisins

- 1/2 cup flat leaf parsley, finely chopped + some for garnish
- a few pinches of cayenne for heat optional
- 8 ounces tempeh, sliced into triangles
- 1/4 tsp liquid smoke optional
- 1 1/2 Tbsp maple syrup, grade B
- 1 tsp extra virgin olive oil or virgin coconut oil
- 2-3 tsp tamari or 2 tsp soy sauce
- salt and pepper for carrot salad - to taste

Directions::

1. Warm a skillet up over high heat and add in the coconut or olive oil.
2. When oil is hot, add the tempeh triangles, tamari, maple and liquid smoke.
3. Flip the tempeh around a bit to allow it to absorb the liquid.

4. Cook for about 5 minutes, flipping the tempeh a few times throughout the cooking process.
5. When tempeh is browned and edges blackened a bit, and all liquid absorbed, turn off heat.
6. Sprinkle the walnut pieces and some black pepper over top the tempeh and set pan aside to keep triangles warm in skillet.
7. In a large mixing bowl, add the carrots, tahini, lemon juice, spices, parsley, maple syrup, optional raisins and onion.
8. Toss very well for a few minutes to marinate the carrots with the dressing. For a creamier salad, add another spoonful of tahini.
9. To thin things out and make the salad zestier, add another splash of lemon juice or a teaspoon of apple cider vinegar. Finally, add salt and pepper to the carrot salad to taste.
10. Pour the carrot salad in a large serving bowl and top with the tempeh.

11. Serve right away or place in the fridge to serve in a few hours or up to a day later. The carrots will soften the longer they set in the fridge.

Bangkok Black Rice Salad

Ingredients:

Salad

- 1 small cucumber about 6 inches, cut into 1/4-inch dice

- 1/2 cup diced red onion

- 1 clove garlic, minced

- 1/2 cup lightly salted and roasted cashew halves and pieces

- 1 cup Thai black rice, simmered gently in 1 3/4 cups water over medium heat, covered, for about 35 minutes—watch closely and add more water or reduce heat if necessary—then cooled

- 1 large peach, pitted, and cut into 1/4-inch dice

- 1 red bell pepper, cut into 1/4-inch dice
- 2 to 3 tablespoons each fresh cilantro leaves, finely chopped mint preferably not spearmint, and finely chopped Thai or Vietnamese basil if you can't find the latter–I grow it so I have it at the ready–just substitute regular basil or omit and use about 1/4 cup each cilantro leaves and finely chopped mint

Dressing

- 2 to 3 tablespoons vegan fish sauce it is sold as "vegetarian" in Asian markets
- Zest and juice of 1/2 of a large lime
- 2 to 3 teaspoons natural sugar
- 1 small medium-hot chili, stemmed, cored, seeds removed, and minced
- Pinch of sea salt or to taste

Directions::

1. In a medium bowl, combine all salad Ingredients:.
2. In a small cup or bowl whisk together all dressing Ingredients:, and check for flavor balance, adding more of any ingredient if you choose.
3. Pour the dressing over the salad, and toss with a fork to combine.
4. Check for salt and adjust if necessary.
5. Serve at room temperature or chilled.

Lentil Salad In Olive Oil

Ingredients:

- 1/2 teaspoon freshly ground cumin seed
- 1/2 teaspoon freshly ground coriander seed
- 1/4 teaspoon freshly ground cardamom seed
- 1/2 teaspoon ground fenugreek
- 1 cup dried brown lentils, picked over and rinsed well
- 1/4 cup extra-virgin olive oil
- 2 large garlic cloves, finely chopped
- Salt
- Fresh ground black pepper

Directions:

1. In a small saucepan, heat 3 tablespoons of the olive oil over medium heat with the garlic.

2. As soon as the garlic begins to sizzle remove from the burner, add the cumin, coriander, cardamom, and fenugreek, stir, and set aside.
3. Place the lentils in a medium saucepan of lightly salted cold water and bring to a boil.
4. Cook until al dente, about 25 minutes from when you turned the heat onor a little longer if you want them softer.
5. Drain and toss with the garlic, olive oil, and spices while still hot.
6. Season with salt and pepper, toss, and arrange on a serving platter. Drizzle the remaining 1 tablespoon olive oil over the top.
7. Serve at room temperature. Enjoy!

Hemp Protein Granola Bars

Ingredients:

- 1/4 cup sesame seeds
- 2 tbsp. Poppy seeds
- 2 tsp. Cinnamon
- 1/2 tsp. Salt
- 3 ripe bananas
- 1/4 cup sunflower oil or coconut, olive, walnut…
- 2 tsp. Vanilla extract
- 3 tbsp. Maple syrup
- 2 tbsp. Chia seeds
- 1 1/2 cups rolled oats
- 3/4 cup walnuts, chopped or any other nut

- 1 cup dates, chopped or any other dried fruit
- 1 cup coconut flakes
- 1/2 cup hemp protein powder
- 6 tbsp. Water

Directions:
1. Preheat oven to 350F.
2. In a small bowl, mix the chia seeds and water together.
3. Set aside.
4. In a large bowl combine the dry Ingredients:.
5. In a food processor or blender, mix bananas, oil, vanilla, and maple syrup you can also just mash everything together with a fork.
6. Add chia gel and pulse to mix.
7. Pour wet Ingredients: over dry Ingredients: and stir until well combined.
8. Spread the batter evenly into a baking pan mine was 9" x 11", and smooth out the top with the back of a spatula.

9. Bake for 20-25 minutes, or until edges are golden brown.
10. Let cool completely, store in airtight container and keep in the refrigerator for longer shelf life.
11. You can also freeze these – take one out half an hour before you want a perfect snack.

Quinoa With Acorn Squash

Ingredients:

- 1/4 cup raisins
- 2 tsp minced fresh parsley
- 2 scallions, green parts only, chopped
- 1/4 cup olive oil, plus more for roasting squash
- 2 tbsp. lemon juice
- Zest of half a lemon
- 3/4 cup of quinoa, cooked
- 1 acorn or kabocha squash
- 3/4 cup pomegranate seeds
- Salt and pepper

Directions:

1. Preheat oven to 400 degrees.
2. Line a baking sheet with aluminum foil.
3. With a sharp knife, cut the top and bottom off the squash.
4. Cut the acorn squash in half lengthwise and, using a spoon, scoop out the seeds.
5. Cut each piece in half again lengthwise.
6. Then slice each quarter lengthwise, creating 1/2 inch slices.
7. Place squash slices into a bowl and drizzle with olive oil and a sprinkle of salt.
8. Spread across the pan and arrange so each piece sits flat.
9. Roast in the oven for 25 minutes.
10. Meanwhile, make the dressing by whisking together the 1/4 cup of olive oil, the lemon juice, lemon zest, parsley, and scallions.
11. Season with salt and pepper, to taste.
12. Once the acorn squash is finished, remove from the oven and let cool for a few minutes.

13. Mix together the cooked quinoa, pomegranate seeds, raisins, and dressing in a big serving bowl.
14. Season with salt and pepper, to taste.
15. Top with roasted squash pieces.

Mellow Lentil Soup

Ingredients:

- 1/2 tsp sea salt
- Freshly ground black pepper to taste
- 3/4-1 tsp mild curry powder
- 1 tsp paprika
- 1/4 tsp dried thyme
- 2 cups dry red lentils, rinsed
- 3 cups vegetable stock
- 3 1/2 - 4 1/2 cups water adjust to desired consistency
- 2-3 tsp fresh rosemary, chopped
- 1 1/2 tbsp. Water
- 1 1/2 cups onion, diced

- 1 cup celery, diced

- 1 cup carrots, diced

- 3 large cloves garlic, minced

- 1/2 tbsp. Apple cider vinegar

Directions:
1. In a large pot on medium heat, add water, onion, celery, carrots, garlic, salt, pepper, curry powder, paprika and dried thyme and stir to combine.
2. Cover and cook for 7-8 minutes, stirring occasionally.
3. Rinse lentils.
4. Add lentils, stock, 3 1/2 cups of the water, and stir to combine.
5. Increase heat to bring mixture to a boil.
6. Add rosemary, reduce heat to low, cover, and simmer for 25 minutes.
7. Add vinegar, and more water as desired to thin the soup.

Vegan Salad

Ingredients:

Salad

- Pitted black olives, ½ cup

- Black pepper, 1 teaspoon

- Sliced grape tomatoes, 1 cup

- Olive oil, 1 tablespoon

- Fresh Apples

- Sliced cauliflower

- Thinly sliced spring onion, ½ cup

- Chopped fresh basil leaves, ½ cup

- Bibb lettuce, one large head

- Sesame seeds

- Salt, ½ teaspoon

Dressing

- Minced garlic, 1 tablespoon

- Lemon juice, 2 tablespoons

- Black pepper, ½ teaspoon

- Salt, ¼ teaspoon

- Water, 1 tablespoon

- Olive oil, 3 tablespoons

Directions:
1. Mix the listed Ingredients: for the salad dressing and refrigerate it while you make the salad.
2. Boil the French style green beans for 5 minutes in hot water and drain the water off.
3. Lay the Bibb lettuce on 4 serving plates.
4. Cover the lettuce with the cooked green beans, dividing them evenly among the 4 plates.

5. Sprinkle the black olives, tomatoes, tofu, and onions on top of the green beans, dividing them evenly among the four plates.
6. Serve the salads with the chilled dressing on the side.

Peppers Stuffed With Veggies

Ingredients:

- Black pepper, ½ teaspoon

- Sliced cherry tomatoes, 1 cup

- Cucumber, ½ peeled and diced

- Fresh parsley, ¼ cup

- Salt, ¼ teaspoon

- Scallions, 4 cleaned and sliced

- Red, Yellow, and Green bell peppers, three cleaned and cut in half

- Balsamic vinegar, 2 tablespoons

- Stalk celery, four washed and diced

- Dijon mustard, 3 tablespoons

- Plain soy yogurt, ½ cup

- Pre-cooked rice if needed

Directions:
1. Blend the soy yogurt, mustard, black pepper, salt, and balsamic vinegar until they are well blended.
2. Put in the scallion slices, tomato slices, and the diced celery and cucumbers and toss these with the liquid dressing.
3. Scoop the Ingredients: into the bell pepper halves.

Cranberry Chickpea Salad

Ingredients:

- Black pepper, 1 teaspoon
- Chopped Avocado
- Red cherry tomatoes, sliced in halves, 1 cup
- Whole cranberries, washed and sliced, 1 cup
- Olive oil, 2 tablespoons
- Fresh parsley, chopped, ¼ cup
- Chopped cucumber, 1 cup
- Salt, ½ teaspoon
- ½ Cup Couscous
- Lemon juice, 2 tablespoons
- Chickpeas drained and rinsed 1 cup
- Thinly sliced red onion, ½ cup

Directions:

1. Pre-cook the couscous and set aside
2. Mix the tomatoes, cucumber, cranberries, chickpeas, and sliced onions in a medium-sized mixing bowl.
3. In another bowl, blend the fresh parsley, salt, black pepper, olive oil, and lemon juice.
4. Mix the couscous with the veggies
5. Pour the lemon juice dressing over the veggies in the larger bowl and mix everything well.

Tofu Scramble 'Eggs'

Ingredients:

- 1 teaspoon of salt
- 1 454g block firm tofu
- 1 tablespoon olive oil
- 1 ½ cup button mushrooms, sliced
- 2 cups of black beans, drained and rinsed
- 1 red bell pepper, chopped
- 2 garlic cloves, minced
- 2 tablespoons nutritional yeast
- 1 teaspoon ground cumin
- ¼ teaspoon garlic powder
- ¼ teaspoon of onion powder
- ¾ teaspoon turmeric

- ½ cup yellow onion, chopped

Directions:

1. Combine all the spices in a bowl.
2. Heat a large skillet over medium heat and add olive oil. Once the oil is hot, add the mushrooms, bell pepper, garlic, and yellow onion. Saute for 10 minutes or until the veggies begin to brown.
3. Add the tofu block and break it apart with a spoon until it obtains a scrambled texture with lots of chunks.
4. Stir in the spice mixture and black beans. Cook for 5 more minutes.
5. Serve with your favorite gluten-free, dairy-free bread, and sliced avocado.

Tempe Sweet Potato Scrambled 'Eggs'

Ingredients:

- ½ cup onions, diced
- 2 garlic cloves, minced
- 1 red bell pepper, diced
- 1 tablespoon soy sauce
- ½ tablespoon lemon juice
- 1 tablespoon maple syrup
- 1 tablespoon smoked paprika
- 1 8-oz package temper, crumbled
- 1 small sweet potato, finely diced
- 2 tablespoons olive oil
- 1 tablespoon ground cumin

Directions:

1. In a large skillet over medium heat, heat the olive oil. Add a sweet potato and saute for 5 minutes or until lightly browned.
2. Add onion and saute until the onion becomes softened or about 5 minutes.
3. Add garlic and saute for 1 more minute. Add tempeh and saute until browned.
4. Add the bell pepper, soy sauce, cumin, paprika, lemon juice, and maple syrup. Saute for 2 more minutes.
5. Serve alongside toasted gluten-free, dairy-free bread or on a tortilla. Can be topped with avocado slices, scallions, and hot sauce.

Chickpea Onion Omelet

Ingredients:

- 8 tablespoon water
- 2 tablespoons olive oil
- ½ cup fresh dill, chopped
- 3 tablespoon chickpea flour
- ½ cup onion, chopped
- Salt and pepper to taste

Directions:
1. Whisk chickpea flour, salt, and pepper will in a medium bowl.
2. Add water and whisk until a creamy butter is formed.
3. Add chopped onions and chopped dill. Mix well.

4. Over medium heat, heat olive oil in a non-stick frying pan. Once the oil is heated, scoop the batter into the pan and spread it around with a spoon so that it forms a round omelets.
5. Cook for 3 minutes. Flip the omelets and cook for 2 more minutes.
6. Remove from the heat and allow to cool for a few minutes. Serve warm alongside your favorite gluten-free, dairy-free bread.

Strawberry Muffins

Ingredients:

- 1 cup whole wheat flour
- 1 teaspoon baking soda
- 1 – 6 ounce container blueberry flavored coconut milk yogurt
- 1 tablespoon vanilla
- 1 tablespoon almond milk
- 6 sliced strawberries
- 3 tablespoons powdered egg replacer
- 1/4 cup water
- 1 cup evaporated cane sugar
- 1 cup blueberry granola

Directions:

1. Preheat oven to 350 F. Prepare a muffin pan with 8 liners.
2. Mix together water and egg replacer in a small bowl. In a large bowl, combine sugar, flour and baking soda. In a separate bowl, combine yogurt, vanilla, and almond milk.
3. Add all wet Ingredients: to dry bowl and stir until just mixed and then gently stir in the strawberries.
4. Divide batter between 8 cupcake liners. Top each muffin with blueberry granola. Bake for 22 minutes or until done.

Carrot Apple Muffins

Ingredients:

- 1 large apple, unpeeled and shredded
- 1/2 cup raisins
- 1/2 cup dried coconut flakes
- 1/2 cup walnuts
- 1 cup all-purpose flour
- 1 cup whole wheat flour
- 2 teaspoons baking soda
- 2 teaspoons cinnamon
- 2 1/2 tablespoons ground flax seed
- 7 tablespoons hot water
- 1/3 cup canola oil
- 2/3 cup nondairy milk

- 2 teaspoons vanilla extract

- 2/3 cup packed brown sugar

- 2 cups carrot, peeled and shredded

- 1/2 teaspoon salt

Directions:

1. Preheat oven to 350 F and line a muffin pan. In a small bowl, whisk together flax seed and hot water to make an egg replacer. Set aside.
2. Pulse the carrots and apple together in a food processor until chopped into very fine pieces, but not pureed.
3. In a large mixing bowl, mix together wet Ingredients:, sugar, carrot, and apple. Stir in remaining Ingredients:, and mix gently until fully incorporated. Try not to over mix.
4. Spoon into prepared muffin tins. Fill according to how big you want your muffins to be. Bake for 25 minutes. Let cool completely before serving.

Banana Muffins

Ingredients:

- 1/2 cup sugar
- 1 teaspoon baking soda
- 1 teaspoon baking powder
- 1/2 teaspoon salt
- 3 mashed bananas
- 1 1/2 cups flour
- 1/3 cup margarine
- Egg substitute 1 egg equivalent

Directions:

1. Mix all Ingredients: well in a medium sized bowl. Pour mixture into muffin tins, bake in the oven at 375 F for 20-25 minutes.

Stuffed Portobello Mushrooms

Ingredients:

- 1 red bell pepper, finely chopped
- 1 zucchini, finely chopped
- 1 cup fresh spinach, chopped
- 1 cup cooked quinoa or rice
- 1/4 cup nutritional yeast
- 2 tablespoons balsamic vinegar
- 1 tablespoon soy sauce or tamari for gluten-free option
- 1 teaspoon dried thyme
- 4 large Portobello mushrooms, stems removed
- 2 tablespoons olive oil

- 1 small onion, finely chopped
- 2 cloves garlic, minced
- Salt and pepper to taste
- Vegan cheese optional, for topping

Directions:

1. Preheat your oven to 375°F 190°C.
2. Clean the Portobello mushrooms by gently wiping them with a damp paper towel. Remove the stems and use a spoon to scrape out the gills from the underside of the mushrooms to create more space for the stuffing.
3. In a large skillet, heat 1 tablespoon of olive oil over medium heat.
4. Add the finely chopped onion and sauté for 2-3 minutes until it becomes translucent.
5. Stir in the minced garlic and cook for an additional 1-2 minutes until the garlic is fragrant.

6. Add the finely chopped red bell pepper and zucchini to the skillet. Sauté the vegetables for about 5 minutes until they become tender.
7. Mix in the chopped fresh spinach and cook for a few more minutes until the spinach wilts.
8. In a large mixing bowl, combine the sautéed vegetables with the cooked quinoa or rice.
9. Stir in the nutritional yeast, balsamic vinegar, soy sauce or tamari, dried thyme, salt, and pepper. Mix everything together until well combined.
10. Drizzle the remaining 1 tablespoon of olive oil over the Portobello mushrooms and rub it on both sides to coat them with the oil.
11. Place the mushrooms on a baking sheet, gill-side up.
12. Divide the stuffing mixture among the mushrooms, pressing it down gently to fill each mushroom cap.

13. If desired, top each stuffed mushroom with vegan cheese for added flavor and creaminess.
14. Bake the Vegan Stuffed Portobello Mushrooms in the preheated oven for about 20-25 minutes, or until the mushrooms are tender and the stuffing is heated through.
15. Serve the mouthwatering Vegan Stuffed Portobello Mushrooms on a plate.
16. Enjoy this savory and satisfying dish as a delightful main course or a hearty side dish, perfect for special occasions or anytime you want to impress with a restaurant-quality vegan meal!

Coconut Curry Noodles

Ingredients:

- 1 zucchini, julienned
- 2 tablespoons red curry paste
- 1 can coconut milk
- 1 tablespoon soy sauce or tamari for gluten-free option
- 1 tablespoon brown sugar or maple syrup
- 1 tablespoon lime juice
- 1 cup vegetable broth
- Salt and pepper to taste
- Fresh cilantro and lime wedges for garnish
- 8 oz 225g rice noodles or any other vegan noodles of your choice

- 1 tablespoon vegetable oil
- 1 small onion, finely chopped
- 2 cloves garlic, minced
- 1 tablespoon fresh ginger, grated
- 1 red bell pepper, thinly sliced
- 1 carrot, julienned
- Crushed red pepper flakes optional, for added heat

Directions:

1. Cook the rice noodles according to the package Directions:until they are al dente. Drain and set aside.
2. In a large skillet or wok, heat the vegetable oil over medium heat.
3. Add the finely chopped onion and sauté for 2-3 minutes until it becomes translucent.

4. Stir in the minced garlic and grated ginger, cooking for an additional 1-2 minutes until they become fragrant.
5. Add the thinly sliced red bell pepper, julienned carrot, and zucchini to the skillet. Stir-fry the vegetables for about 3-4 minutes until they start to soften.
6. Spoon the red curry paste into the skillet with the vegetables, stirring well to coat them with the aromatic paste.
7. Pour in the coconut milk, soy sauce or tamari, brown sugar or maple syrup, and lime juice. Mix everything together until well combined.
8. Stir in the vegetable broth to create a flavorful and creamy coconut curry sauce.
9. Let the sauce simmer for about 5-7 minutes, allowing the flavors to meld and the vegetables to become tender.

10. Season the Vegan Coconut Curry Noodles with salt and pepper to taste. Adjust the seasonings according to your preferences.
11. Add the cooked rice noodles to the skillet, tossing them with the coconut curry sauce and vegetables until they are well coated.
12. Serving:
13. Serve the aromatic and creamy Vegan Coconut Curry Noodles in bowls.
14. Garnish with fresh cilantro and lime wedges, if desired, for added freshness and a burst of citrusy flavor.
15. For those who enjoy spicier dishes, you can sprinkle some crushed red pepper flakes over the noodles for an extra kick of heat.
16. Enjoy this delicious and comforting noodle dish as a delightful lunch or dinner, perfect for satisfying your craving for Thai-inspired flavors and creamy coconut goodness!

Roasted Brussels Sprouts With Balsamic Glaze

Ingredients:

- 2 tablespoons balsamic vinegar
- 1 tablespoon maple syrup or agave nectar
- 1/4 teaspoon garlic powder
- 1/4 teaspoon dried thyme optional, for added flavor
- Crushed red pepper flakes optional, for a hint of heat
- 1 lb 450g Brussels sprouts, trimmed and halved
- 2 tablespoons olive oil
- Salt and pepper to taste
- Fresh parsley, chopped, for garnish optional

Directions:

1. Preheat your oven to 400°F 200°C.
2. In a large mixing bowl, toss the halved Brussels sprouts with olive oil, salt, and pepper until they are well coated.
3. Spread the Brussels sprouts evenly on a baking sheet lined with parchment paper or a silicone baking mat.
4. Roast the Brussels sprouts in the preheated oven for about 20-25 minutes, or until they become tender and crispy at the edges. Toss them halfway through the roasting time for even cooking.
5. While the Brussels sprouts are roasting, prepare the balsamic glaze. In a small saucepan, combine the balsamic vinegar, maple syrup or agave nectar, garlic powder, and dried thyme if using. Bring the mixture to a simmer over low heat.
6. Let the glaze simmer for about 3-4 minutes, stirring occasionally, until it thickens slightly

and develops a syrupy consistency. Remove the glaze from heat and set it aside.
7. Once the Brussels sprouts are done roasting, transfer them to a serving dish.
8. Drizzle the balsamic glaze over the roasted Brussels sprouts, tossing them gently to coat them with the sweet and tangy glaze.
9. If desired, sprinkle some crushed red pepper flakes over the glazed Brussels sprouts for a touch of spiciness.
10. Serve the mouthwatering Vegan Roasted Brussels Sprouts with Balsamic Glaze on a platter.
11. Garnish with chopped fresh parsley, if desired, for added freshness and a burst of herbaceous flavor.
12. Enjoy this delectable and flavorful side dish as a delightful accompaniment to any meal, whether it's a festive holiday feast or a simple weeknight dinner!

Chickpea And Spinach Curry

Ingredients:

- Tomatoes, diced
- Onion, chopped
- Garlic, minced
- Ginger, grated
- Curry spices cumin, coriander, turmeric, garam masala
- Coconut milk
- Chickpeas, cooked
- Spinach, fresh or frozen
- Lemon juice

Directions:
1. Sauté onions, garlic, and ginger until fragrant.
2. Add diced tomatoes and cook until softened.

3. Stir in chickpeas, spinach, and curry spices.
4. Pour in coconut milk and simmer until flavors meld.
5. Finish with a squeeze of lemon juice.

Lentil Walnut Loaf

Ingredients:

- Onion, finely chopped
- Garlic, minced
- Tomato paste
- Oats gluten-free
- Flaxseed meal as a binder
- Green or brown lentils, cooked
- Walnuts, chopped
- Carrots, grated
- BBQ glaze

Directions:

1. Mash cooked lentils and mix with chopped walnuts, grated carrots, onions, garlic, tomato paste, oats, and flaxseed meal.

2. Form into a loaf shape and bake until firm.
3. Glaze with your favorite gluten-free, vegan BBQ sauce.

Teriyaki Tofu Stir-Fry

Ingredients:

- Bell peppers, sliced
- Carrots, julienned
- Teriyaki sauce
- Sesame oil
- Extra-firm tofu, pressed and cubed
- Broccoli florets
- Scallions, chopped
- Sesame seeds

Directions:

1. Sauté tofu cubes until golden brown.
2. Add broccoli, bell peppers, and carrots, stirring in teriyaki sauce and sesame oil.
3. Cook until vegetables are tender-crisp.

4. Garnish with chopped scallions and sesame seeds.

Traditional Miso Ramen With Silken Tofu

Ingredients:

- 2 tbsp soy sauce
- 1 tbsp sesame oil
- 1 block silken tofu, cubed
- 2 cups baby spinach
- 3 green onions, sliced
- 9 oz ramen noodles
- 4 cups vegetable broth
- 1/3 cup white miso paste
- Nori sheets for garnish

Directions:

1. Cook ramen noodles according to package Directions::. Drain and set aside.

2. In a pot, whisk together vegetable broth, miso paste, soy sauce, and sesame oil. Simmer for 15 minutes.
3. Add cubed silken tofu and baby spinach to the broth. Cook until spinach wilts.
4. Divide noodles into bowls, ladle hot broth over them, and top with sliced green onions and nori sheets.

Red Curry Miso Ramen With Roasted Cauliflower

Ingredients:

- 1/4 cup red miso paste
- 2 tbsp red curry paste
- 1 tbsp soy sauce
- 1 tbsp sesame oil
- 1 cup coconut milk
- 1 red bell pepper, sliced
- 10 oz ramen noodles
- 1 small cauliflower, cut into florets
- 4 cups vegetable broth
- Fresh cilantro for garnish

Directions:

1. Cook ramen noodles according to package Directions:::. Drain and set aside.
2. Roast cauliflower florets in the oven until golden brown.
3. In a pot, whisk together vegetable broth, red miso paste, red curry paste, soy sauce, sesame oil, and coconut milk. Simmer for 15 minutes.
4. Add roasted cauliflower and sliced red bell pepper to the broth. Cook until vegetables are tender.
5. Divide noodles into bowls, ladle hot broth over them, and garnish with fresh cilantro.

Peanut Miso Ramen With Spinach And Crispy Shallots

Ingredients:

- 2 tbsp peanut butter
- 1 tbsp soy sauce
- 1 tbsp sesame oil
- 2 cups baby spinach
- 3 shallots, thinly sliced and fried until crispy
- 8 oz ramen noodles
- 4 cups vegetable broth
- 1/3 cup white miso paste
- Crushed peanuts for garnish

Directions:

1. Cook ramen noodles according to package Directions::. Drain and set aside.

2. In a pot, whisk together vegetable broth, miso paste, peanut butter, soy sauce, and sesame oil. Simmer for 15 minutes.
3. Add baby spinach to the broth. Cook until wilted.
4. Divide noodles into bowls, ladle hot broth over them, and top with crispy shallots and crushed peanuts.

Chocolate-Covered Strawberries

Ingredients:

- Fresh strawberries

- Dark, milk, or white chocolate chopped or in chip form

- Optional: Sprinkles, chopped nuts, coconut flakes for garnish

Directions:

1. Wash and thoroughly dry the strawberries.
2. Melt the chocolate in a microwave-safe basin, stirring every 30 seconds until smooth.
3. Hold each strawberry by the stem and dip it into the melted chocolate, covering it in half or totally.
4. Place the dipped strawberries on a parchment-lined tray.
5. Optional: While the chocolate is still wet, sprinkle the garnishes over the strawberries.

6. Refrigerate until the chocolate sets, then enjoy these delectable Chocolate-Covered Strawberries.

Banana Chocolate Chip Cookies

Ingredients:

- 2 ripe bananas, mashed 1 1/2 cups rolled oats
- 1/4 cup chocolate chips
- Optional: 1/4 cup chopped nuts, 1/2 teaspoon vanilla extract

Directions:

1. In a bowl, mix the mashed bananas, rolled oats, chocolate chips, and any extra additions.
2. Mix until completely blended.
3. Scoop spoonfuls of the mixture onto the prepared baking sheet.
4. Flatten the cookies gently with the back of a spoon.
5. Bake for 12-15 minutes until golden brown.\
6. Let the Banana Chocolate Chip Cookies cool before savoring these lovely, naturally sweet sweets.

Berry Nice Cream

Ingredients:

- 2 cups frozen mixed berries strawberries, blueberries, raspberries
- 2 ripe bananas, cut and frozen
- Optional: Splash of almond milk or coconut milk for creaminess

Directions:
1. In a blender or food processor, mix the frozen berries and bananas.
2. Add a dash of almond or coconut milk if required.
3. Blend till smooth and creamy, approximating ice cream consistency.
4. Serve immediately as a delightful and guilt-free Berry Nice Cream dessert.
5. These Sweet Indulgences give a lovely retreat into the realm of seductive sweetness.

Whether it's the exquisite simplicity of Chocolate-Covered Strawberries, the healthy appeal of Banana Chocolate Chip Cookies, or the refreshing Berry Nice Cream, each delight encourages you to appreciate moments of pure pleasure.

6. Enjoy these delicious treats that are as appealing to the palette as they are to the spirit.

Peanut Noodle Salad

Ingredients:

For the salad:

- 8 oz. Rice Noodles
- ½ of 1 Red Bell Pepper, sliced thinly
- 2 Scallions, chopped
- ½ tsp. Black Sesame Seeds
- 1 cup Carrots, shredded
- 1/3 cup Peanuts, chopped

For the peanut dressing:

- 3 tbsp. Sriracha
- 2 tbsp. Hot Water
- 2 Garlic cloves, minced
- 1/3 cup Peanut Butter, creamy

- 1 tbsp. Rice Vinegar

Directions:

1. First, cook the noodles by following the Directions: given on the packet.
2. Drain the excess water and then rinse it under cold water. Keep aside.
3. After that, combine all the Ingredients: needed to make the dressing in a small bowl until mixed well. Set it aside.
4. Mix the noodles with all the remaining Ingredients: and dressing.
5. Combine and then place in the refrigerator until you're ready to serve.

Broccoli Edam Me Salad

Ingredients:

For the salad:

- ½ cup Peanuts

- Sesame Seeds, as needed, for garnishing

- ½ cup Green onion, sliced thinly

- 1 Broccoli head, large & torn into florets

- 1 cup Edam me, shelled & cooked

For the peanut sauce:

- 1 tbsp. Rice Vinegar

- 2 tbsp. Hot Water

- ¼ cup Peanut Butter, natural

- 1/8 tsp. Sesame Oil, toasted

- 1 tbsp. Soy Sauce

- 1 tbsp. Agave Nectar

Directions:

1. To make this easy salad, you first need to heat water in a large pot over medium heat.
2. Once it starts boiling, stir in the broccoli and cook for half a minute.
3. After that, transfer the cooked broccoli to a strainer and place in a bowl of cold water.
4. Drain the broccoli and put in a large mixing bowl.
5. Add all the remaining salad Ingredients: to the bowl and toss well.
6. Now, make the peanut sauce by mixing all the Ingredients: needed to make the dressing in a bowl with a whisk. Set it aside.
7. Finally, spoon in the dressing and garnish it with the sesame seeds.

Arugula Green Beans Salad

Ingredients:

For the salad:

- 2 handful of Arugula

- 4 tbsp. Capers

- 15 oz. Lentils, cooked

- 15 oz. Green Kidney Beans

For the dressing:

- 1 tbsp. Caper Brine

- 1 tbsp. Tahini

- 2 tbsp. Hot Sauce

- 1 tbsp. Balsamic Vinegar

- 1 tbsp. Tamari

- 2 tbsp. Peanut Butter

Directions:

1. Begin by placing all the Ingredients: needed to make the dressing in a medium bowl and whisk it well until combined.
2. After that, combine the arugula, capers, kidney beans, and lentils in a large bowl. Pour the dressing over it.
3. Serve and enjoy.

Vegan Keto Chili

Ingredients:

- 1 cup of cauliflower rice
- One can 14 oz diced tomatoes
- One can 14 oz tomato sauce
- One can 14 oz black soybeans, drained and rinsed
- 2 tbsp. tomato paste
- 2 tbsp. chilli powder
- 1 tsp cumin
- 1 tsp paprika
- Salt and pepper to taste
- Avocado, sliced, for garnish
- 1 tbsp. olive oil

- One onion, diced
- Three cloves garlic, minced
- One bell pepper, diced
- Two zucchinis, diced
- Fresh cilantro, chopped, for garnish

Directions:
1. In a big saucepan, warm the olive oil over medium heat.
2. Toss in some minced garlic, diced bell pepper, and chopped onion. Saute the veggies in oil until they're tender.
3. Include rice made from cauliflower and sliced zucchini. Keep cooking for a further three to five minutes.
4. Add the black soybeans, tomato paste, chopped tomatoes, tomato sauce, cumin, paprika, salt, and pepper. Stir in the chilli powder.

5. Turn the heat down to low and simmer the chilli for 20 to 30 minutes to combine the flavor's.
6. Tailor the seasoning to your liking.
7. Top the vegan keto chilli with chopped cilantro and sliced avocado.

Eggplant Lasagna Rolls

Ingredients:

- 1 cup of spinach, chopped
- 1 cup of marinara sauce
- 1 cup of shredded mozzarella cheese
- 1/4 cup of grated Parmesan cheese
- Salt and pepper to taste
- Two medium-sized eggplants, thinly sliced lengthwise
- 1 cup of ricotta cheese
- Fresh basil for garnish

Directions:

1. Get your oven preheated to 375°F, which is 190°C.

2. Roast the eggplant slices for 10 to 15 minutes, or until tender, after brushing them with olive oil and seasoning them with salt and pepper.
3. The ricotta cheese and chopped spinach should be combined in a bowl.
4. Top each eggplant slice with a tbsp of the ricotta mixture.
5. Roll up the eggplant slices with the seam side down in a baking dish.
6. Top the rolls with mozzarella and Parmesan cheese and drizzle with marinara sauce.
7. Please put it in the oven, let it melt, and bubble for twenty to twenty-five minutes.
8. Before serving, top with fresh basil.

Almond-Crusted Tofu Nuggets

Ingredients:

- 1 tsp onion powder

- 1/2 tsp paprika

- Salt and pepper to taste

- 2 tbsp. almond milk

- One block of extra-firm tofu pressed and cut into nuggets

- 1 cup of almond flour

- 1 tsp garlic powder

- Cooking spray or oil for baking

Directions:

1. Turn the oven on high heat 400°F, 200°C.
2. Combine almond flour, onion and garlic powders, paprika, salt, and pepper in a bowl.

3. Before coating the tofu nuggets with the almond flour mixture, dip them in almond milk.
4. On a parchment-lined baking sheet, arrange the coated nuggets.
5. To get a golden brown and crispy texture, bake for 20 to 25 minutes.
6. Halfway through cooking, turn the nuggets over to ensure equal browning.

Red Curry Quinoa Fried Rice

Ingredients:

- 1 inch ginger, chopped
- 1 medium yellow onion, chopped
- 1 large carrot, cut into rounds
- 1 large red pepper, chopped into 1/2 inch
- 1 cup broccoli florets, small
- 1/4 cup green peas frozen
- 2 tablespoons red curry paste
- 2 teaspoons soy sauce
- 1/4 teaspoon salt or to taste
- 1/4 cup Thai basil, chopped
- 2-3 stalks green onion, chopped
- 1 cup quinoa

- 1 cup coconut milk

- 1/2 cup water

- 1.5 tablespoons oil vegetable or avocado

- 3-4 large garlic cloves, chopped

- 1 small lime, juice of

Directions:

1. Rinse quinoa and cook in the Instant Pot with coconut milk and water on high pressure for 2 minutes. Allow natural pressure release.
2. Saute garlic, ginger, and onion in oil. Add veggies and cook for 3 minutes.
3. Add curry paste, soy sauce, salt, and cooked quinoa. Stir well.
4. Unplug the Instant Pot, add Thai basil, green onion, and lime juice.
5. Serve with a side of hot sauce.

Alfredo Sauce

Ingredients:

- 3/4 cup raw cashews
- 3 cups vegetable broth
- 1/2-1 teaspoon salt, to taste
- 1 pound 16-oz cooked fettuccine pasta whole grain or gluten-free if needed
- 2 tablespoons olive oil
- 8 cloves garlic, minced
- 6 cups cauliflower florets fresh or frozen
- Optional: steamed broccoli, kale, or green peas

Directions:

1. Push the sauté feature on the Instant Pot. Add olive oil and minced garlic, cook for a minute or two until fragrant.
2. Turn off sauté, add cauliflower, cashews, and vegetable broth. Cook on high manual pressure for 3 minutes, ensuring it's sealed for pressure buildup.
3. Once done, release the pressure carefully. Transfer to a blender, add salt, and blend until smooth. Pour over pasta and stir. Adjust consistency with water if needed. Serve with optional steamed veggies.
4. In a large pot, sauté garlic in olive oil until fragrant. Add cauliflower, cashews, and vegetable broth. Bring to a boil and cook for 10-15 minutes.
5. Transfer to a blender and blend until smooth. Return to the pot, add salt, and serve.

Mac And Cheese

Ingredients:

- 1 cup potato, peeled & chopped
- ½ cup carrots, peeled & chopped
- 2 garlic cloves, minced
- 2 tablespoons vegan butter
- ¼ cup water
- 16 oz dried elbow macaroni
- 1 tablespoon olive oil
- 4 cups water
- ½ cup raw cashews

For the Sauce

- ½ teaspoon paprika
- 3 tablespoons nutritional yeast

- 2 ½ tablespoons tapioca flour or corn starch
- 2 tablespoons fresh lemon juice
- 1 cup unsweetened almond milk
- ¾ cup vegetable broth
- 1 teaspoon onion powder
- 1 ½ teaspoon salt

Directions:
1. In the pressure cooker, combine elbow macaroni, olive oil, and enough water to cover the pasta.
2. Place a trivet on top of the pasta and set a cake pan on the trivet.
3. In the cake pan, add cashews, potato, carrots, garlic, vegan butter, and ¼ cup water. Cover with foil.
4. Close the pressure cooker lid, ensuring the vent is closed.
5. Cook at high pressure for 4 minutes.

6. Quick release the pressure.
7. Carefully remove the cake pan and pour all Ingredients: into a blender. Add sauce Ingredients: and blend until smooth.
8. Pour the sauce back into the pressure cooker with the noodles, stir until it thickens.
9. Enjoy!

Quinoa Salad With Creamy Balsamic Dressing

Ingredients:

Creamy balsamic dressing

- 1 tbsp maple syrup

- 1/2 cup balsamic vinegar

- 3/4 cup olive oil

- 2 sprigs fresh rosemary approx. 1 1/2 tbsp

- 1/2 tsp sea salt

- 1 shallot

- 2 cloves garlic

- 1/2 cup chopped red bell pepper

- 1 tbsp lemon juice

- 1 tbsp dijon mustard

- pinch of pepper

Quinoa

- 1 cup quinoa, rinsed
- 2 cups water
- 1/2 cup cherry tomatoes, halved
- 1/2 cup asparagus, chopped,
- 1/2 cup sliced carrots
- 1 head broccoli, chopped

Directions:

Creamy balsamic dressing

1. Blend all Ingredients: in a high speed blender until smooth and creamy.
2. There will be extra dressing- use on salads, or steamed veggies, etc.

Quinoa

3. In a saucepan, bring quinoa and water to a boil. Reduce heat to low, and simmer for 15

minutes. Remove from heat, and fluff with a fork.
4. While quinoa is cooking, steam asparagus, carrots, and broccoli until tender.
5. Combine quinoa, and vegetables and toss with 1/2 cup dressing. Enjoy warm or cold.

Sprouted Mung Bean Salad

Ingredients:

- 1/2 cup extra virgin olive oil
- 1 tablespoon muchi curry or any curry paste or sauce
- 1 pinch cayenne pepper
- 2 1/2 tablespoons soy sauce
- 1 tablespoon minced garlic
- 10 cups sprouted mung beans try to use organic
- 1 bunch cilantro, leaves only
- 1/2 cup lemon juice
- 1 tablespoon stone ground mustard

Directions:

1. Toss all of the Ingredients: together in a large serving bowl.
2. Serve immediately.

Black & White Bean Quinoa Salad

Ingredients:

Salad

- 1 cup 250 mL diced cucumbers

- ¼ cup 50 mL diced red onion

- 1 jalapeno pepper, seeded and minced I've never used it and find the dish spicy enough for me, but feel free to add it if you like things hot!

- ¼ cup 50 mL chopped fresh coriander cilantro

- ⅓ cup 75 mL quinoa

- 1 can 19 oz/540 mL black beans, drained and rinsed

- 1 can 19 oz/540 mL navy beans, drained and rinsed

Dressing

- ½ tsp 2 mL chili powder
- 1 tsp 5 mL ground coriander
- ½ tsp 2 mL dried oregano
- ¼ tsp 1 mL salt
- ¼ tsp 1 mL pepper
- ¼ cup 50 mL vegetable oil I use cold pressed extra-virgin olive oil
- 2 tbsp 25 mL lime juice
- 1 tbsp 15 mL cider vinegar
- 1 clove garlic, minced

Directions:

1. In saucepan of boiling salted ⅔ C water, cook quinoa until tender, about 12 minutes. Drain and rinse.

2. Dressing: In large bowl, whisk together oil, lime juice, vinegar, garlic, chili powder, coriander, oregano, salt and pepper.
3. Add quinoa, black beans, navy beans, cucumber, onion, jalapeño pepper and coriander; toss to combine.

Lemony Blueberry Oatmeal

Ingredients:

- 1/2 cup steel-cut oats
- 2 cups Unsweetened So Delicious Coconut Milk
- 1 cup blueberries
- 1 teaspoon vanilla extract
- 1/4 teaspoon lemon extract or 1/2 teaspoon lemon zest
- 1 – 2 tablespoons sweetener
- For serving: finely grated lemon zest and more fresh blueberries

Directions:

1. The night before: Spray your crock with some oil to help with clean up later. Add everything

except sweetener and lemon zest. Cook on low over night 7 to 9 hours.
2. In the morning: Stir your oatmeal well. It may seem watery at the top but if stirred it should become a more uniform consistency. If you used fresh blueberries they will have floated to the top of the crock. Just smash them a little with the spoon while you're mixing the pot to incorporate them into the mix. Stir in sweetener.
3. Top each serving with lemon zest and more fresh blueberries if you want.

Tomato Toast With Balsamic Drizzle

Ingredients:

- Olive oil
- 2 small heirloom tomatoes, thinly sliced
- ½ a ripe avocado
- ¼ cup fresh basil, chopped
- Sea salt
- ½ cup balsamic vinegar
- 2-3 slices hearty, seeded bread
- Black pepper

Directions:

1. Make the balsamic reduction by adding the balsamic vinegar to a small saucepan over medium-high heat.

2. Bring the balsamic to a boil, whisking constantly.
3. Reduce heat and simmer for 10-15 minutes or until balsamic has reduced by half and is thick enough to coat the back of a spoon.
4. Make sure you keep an eye on it – it burns quickly.
5. Slather each slice of bread with a drizzle of olive oil and toast.
6. Evenly divide the avocado between the pieces of toast and use the back of a fork to smash the avocado.
7. Layer the sliced tomatoes on top, sprinkle with fresh basil, and drizzle with the balsamic reduction.
8. Garnish with sea salt and black pepper.
9. Serve immediately.

Miso Maple Tofu Steaks

Ingredients:

- 2 Tbsp. warm water
- 1 tsp ginger, minced
- 1 Tbsp. maple syrup
- 1 tsp tamari
- 2 Tbsp. cilantro, chopped
- 1 block extra-firm tofu
- 3 tsp virgin coconut oil
- 1 Tbsp. white miso paste
- 1 Tbsp. black sesame seeds

Directions:

1. Take the tofu out of the package; place it on a plate or cutting board between two paper

towels. Place a can of tomatoes on top of the tofu to drain excess water for about 2 minutes.
2. While tofu is draining, in a bowl mix miso, water, ginger, maple syrup and tamari together.
3. Heat a skillet on medium-high heat, add coconut oil and swirl around.
4. Slice the tofu into rectangular "steaks" and add them to the skillet, lightly browning each side, about 1 minute per side.
5. Once browned, turn heat to medium-low and add in the marinade over the tofu. If the marinade has firmed up, pour a little more warm water into the mixture and stir until loose.
6. Cook on each side for about 6 minutes.
7. Take off of heat and sprinkle with black sesame seeds and fresh cilantro.

Butternut Squash Slaw

Ingredients:

- 1 lb.s butternut squash, peeled, grated on box grater
- ½ bunch flat-leaf parsley, leaves chopped
- 2 tbsp. Dried cherries, chopped
- ¼ cup sunflower seeds, toasted
- 2 tbsp. Maple syrup
- 2 tbsp. Vegetable oil
- 3 tbsp. Sherry vinegar
- Kosher salt and coarsely ground black pepper

Directions:

1. Whisk together the maple syrup, vegetable oil and sherry vinegar in a large bowl.

2. Add the squash, parsley, dried cherries and sunflower seeds; toss well. Season to taste with salt and pepper.
3. Let sit for 30 minutes at room temperature or 1 hour in the refrigerator before serving.

Thai Soup

Ingredients:

- Lime juice, 2 tablespoons
- Button mushrooms
- Sliced fresh tomato
- Red onion, cut in julienne strips, ½ cup
- Tamari, 1 tablespoon
- Whole Thai chili, 1 tablespoon
- Firm tofu. Pressed and chopped into cubes, ten ounces
- Red bell pepper, 1 cut in julienne strips
- Fresh cilantro coriander, chopped, ½ cup
- Canned coconut milk, one fourteen-ounce size
- Minced garlic, 2 tablespoons

- Ground ginger, 1 tablespoon

- Vegetable broth, 2 cups

Directions:
1. Set a large soup pot on high heat and blend the coconut milk and the veggie broth.
2. Let the liquid boil.
3. Stir in the minced garlic, ground ginger, red bell pepper, sliced onion, Thai chili, and the sliced mushrooms and mix well.
4. Boil the soup for 5 minutes.
5. Stir in the chopped tofu and cook for 5 minutes.
6. Move the pot off the heat and blend in the lime juice, tamari, and cilantro.
7. Let the soup sit for 5 minutes for the flavors to blend.

Zucchini Soup

Ingredients:

- Steam Broccoli for garnishing
- Salt, ½ teaspoon
- Black pepper, 1 cup
- Minced garlic, 4 tablespoons
- Yellow onion, one diced
- Fresh zucchini, two large peeled and sliced
- Vegetable broth, 4 cups
- Fresh basil, 1/3 cup
- Olive oil, 2 tablespoons

Directions:

1. Warm in a large skillet the olive oil over medium heat.

2. Fry the diced onion, minced garlic, and the sliced zucchini for five minutes while stirring often.
3. Stir in the broth and simmer this for 15 minutes.
4. Stir in the salt and black pepper.
5. Put the soup Ingredients: in the blender and puree until it is smooth and creamy.
6. Pour the soup back into the skillet and let it become warm again.

Butternut Squash With Mustard Vinaigrette

Ingredients:

- Black pepper, 1 teaspoon
- Olive oil, 4 tablespoons
- Dry mustard, 1 tablespoon
- Fresh parsley, chopped, ¼ cup
- Butternut squash, 3 small ones peeled, cut in half, and seeded
- Salt, ½ teaspoon
- Apple cider vinegar, 1 tablespoon
- Shallots, 8 cut into wedges

Directions:

1. Heat the oven to 350 F.
2. Smear the inside of the squash with the olive oil and season them with salt and pepper.

3. Set a piece of parchment paper or aluminum foil on a baking sheet.
4. Lay the squash halves on the baking sheet with the inside facing up.
5. Put the slices of shallots on the baking pan around the squash.
6. Bake this for 50 minutes.
7. Blend the fresh parsley, dry mustard, and apple cider vinegar for the vinaigrette.
8. Place the baked squash and shallots on a serving plate and drizzle them with the vinaigrette.

Keto Vanilla Pancakes

Ingredients:

- ¼ cup oat flour
- 1 teaspoon coconut sugar
- 1 tablespoon ground flax seed
- ¼ teaspoon baking powder
- ¼ teaspoon vanilla extract
- ½ scoop vanilla protein powder
- ½ cup coconut milk

Directions:

1. Grease and preheat your waffle iron according to manufacturer's Directions:::.
2. In a large bowl, add the oat flour, vanilla protein powder, sugar, and ground flax seed. Mix well.

3. In a medium bowl, add the flaxseed, baking powder, vanilla extract and ¼ cup of coconut milk. Whisk well and let sit for 5 minutes so that the mixture gels up.
4. Add the wet mixture to the dry Ingredients:. Pour in the remaining coconut milk as well. Stir so that a thick batter is formed.
5. Cook according to your waffle irons manufacturer Directions: until all the batter is used up.
6. Can be frozen for up to two weeks in an airtight container or stored in an airtight container in the refrigerator for a few days. To reheat, simply toast in a toaster, top up with your favorite toppings and enjoy!

Keto-Friendly Vegan Cauliflower Hash Browns

Ingredients:

- 1 teaspoon coconut oil
- ⅓ cup onion chopped
- ½ teaspoon garlic powder
- ½ teaspoon salt
- 2 cups cauliflower florets
- ¼ cup chickpea flour
- 1 tablespoon cornstarch
- 2 tablespoons water if needed

Directions:
1. Preheat your oven to 400 degrees F.
2. Prepare a baking sheet by lining it with parchment paper and brushing the parchment paper with coconut oil.

3. Add the cauliflower and onion to a food processor and pulse until a crumbly texture is achieved. Transfer this mixture to a large bowl.
4. Add the chickpea flour, cornstarch, garlic powder, salt, and water. Only add water if the batter is not moist enough to be pliable.
5. Most times, the moisture from the cauliflower is sufficient. Stir and mix well.
6. Divide this batter into 6 equal portions and shape into 3 x 2 inch patties.
7. Place the patties on the prepared baking sheet and bake for 40 minutes. Turn halfway through the baking process.
8. Allow the hash browns to sit on the baking sheet for 10 minutes after removing from the oven so that they get firmer. Serve with your favorite keto vegan dipping sauce.

Simple Coconut Keto Vegan Pancakes

Ingredients:

- 1 tablespoon unsweetened almond butter
- 1 tablespoon ground flaxseed
- ½ teaspoon baking powder
- 1 tablespoon coconut flour
- 1 cup unsweetened coconut milk
- Canola oil for frying

Directions:

1. In a small bowl, combine almond butter and coconut milk.
2. In a medium bowl, combine the rest of the Ingredients:.
3. Pour the milk mixture into the dry Ingredients: and thoroughly mix.

4. Allow the batter to sit for 5 minutes so that the flaxseed can form a gel and the coconut flour can absorb the water. If this step is skipped, the pancakes will fall apart once cooked.
5. Heat a nonstick frying pan over medium heat. Add the canola oil and spoon the batter into the pan once the oil has heated. Spread the batter around so that it forms 4 inch pancakes.
6. Cook for up to 5 minutes or until the pancakes flip easily and bubbles form on the top. Cook for another 2 minutes or until the underside becomes golden brown.
7. Serve by topping with coconut cream, vegan butter or fresh berries.

Strawberry Applesauce Muffins

Ingredients:

- 2 1/2 cups white whole wheat flour
- 2 cups turbinado sugar
- 1 cup whole wheat flour
- 1 cup rolled oats
- 2 teaspoons baking soda
- 1 teaspoon salt
- 1 cup diced strawberries
- 2 cups soy milk
- 3/4 cup unsweetened applesauce
- 2 tablespoons white vinegar
- 4 teaspoons vanilla extract
- cooking spray

Directions:

1. Preheat oven to 350 degrees F 175 degrees C. Grease 2 muffin tins with cooking spray.
2. Mix soy milk, applesauce, vinegar, and vanilla extract together in a bowl.
3. Sift white whole wheat flour and whole wheat flour together into a separate bowl.
4. Add oats, baking soda, and salt in a separate bowl. Mix in soy milk mixture until smooth. Let batter sit for 5 minutes.
5. Fold strawberries into the batter. Fill muffin tins 2/3 full of batter.
6. Bake in the preheated oven until muffin tops are brown and sides pull away from the tin, 30 to 40 minutes.

Lemon Squares

Ingredients:

Crust:

- 1 cup all-purpose flour
- 5 tablespoons margarine
- 1/4 cup granulated sugar

Filling:

- 1/2 teaspoon baking powder
- 1/8 teaspoon salt
- 2 lemons, zested and juiced
- 3 egg replacers
- 3/4 cup granulated sugar
- 3 tablespoons all-purpose flour
- 1 teaspoon real vanilla

- powdered sugar, optional

Directions:

1. Preheat oven to 350 degrees F.

To make crust:

2. In a bowl, combine crust Ingredients: and press into 8 X 8 inch pan. Bake for 15 minutes.

To make filling:

3. While crust is baking, beat the egg replacers in a bowl until foamy. Add the remainder of the filling Ingredients: and mix together. Pour over the crust, and bake 20 minutes, or until set.

Quinoa Salad

Ingredients:

- 1/2 cup Kalamata olives, pitted and halved
- 1/4 cup fresh parsley, chopped
- 1/4 cup fresh mint, chopped
- 1/4 cup fresh basil, chopped
- 1/4 cup extra-virgin olive oil
- 2 tablespoons lemon juice
- 2 cloves garlic, minced
- 1 teaspoon Dijon mustard
- Salt and pepper to taste
- 1 cup quinoa, rinsed
- 2 cups water or vegetable broth
- 1 cup cherry tomatoes, halved

- 1 cucumber, diced
- 1 red bell pepper, diced
- 1/4 cup red onion, finely chopped
- Vegan feta cheese, crumbled optional, for topping

Directions:

1. In a medium saucepan, combine the rinsed quinoa and water or vegetable broth. Bring to a boil over medium-high heat.
2. Reduce the heat to low, cover the saucepan, and let the quinoa simmer for about 15-20 minutes, or until all the water is absorbed and the quinoa is fluffy and fully cooked.
3. Remove the quinoa from the heat and let it cool slightly.
4. In a large mixing bowl, combine the cooked quinoa, halved cherry tomatoes, diced cucumber, diced red bell pepper, finely chopped red onion, and halved Kalamata olives.
5. Toss in the fresh chopped parsley, mint, and basil to add a burst of herbaceous flavors to the salad.
6. In a small bowl, whisk together the extra-virgin olive oil, lemon juice, minced garlic, and

Dijon mustard to create a zesty and tangy dressing.
7. Drizzle the dressing over the quinoa and vegetable mixture, tossing everything together until the salad is well coated with the flavorful dressing.
8. Season the Vegan Mediterranean Quinoa Salad with salt and pepper to taste. Adjust the seasonings according to your preferences.
9. For added creaminess and tang, you can crumble some vegan feta cheese over the salad, if desired.
10. Serving:
11. Serve the delightful and refreshing Vegan Mediterranean Quinoa Salad in bowls or on a platter.
12. Enjoy this wholesome and nutrient-packed salad as a satisfying lunch or a light dinner, perfect for warm days or whenever you're craving a taste of the Mediterranean!

Jackfruit Tacos With Mango Salsa

Ingredients:

For the Jackfruit Filling:

- 3 cloves garlic, minced
- 1 teaspoon ground cumin
- 1/2 teaspoon smoked paprika
- 1/2 teaspoon chili powder
- 1/4 teaspoon cayenne pepper optional, for added heat
- Salt and pepper to taste
- 1/2 cup vegetable broth
- 1/4 cup barbecue sauce vegan
- 2 cans 20 oz young green jackfruit in brine, drained and rinsed
- 2 tablespoons olive oil

- 1 small onion, finely chopped
- 2 tablespoons lime juice

For the Mango Salsa:

- 1/4 cup diced red onion
- 1 jalapeño, seeded and finely chopped optional, for added heat
- 1/4 cup fresh cilantro, chopped
- 2 tablespoons lime juice
- 1 ripe mango, diced
- 1/2 cup diced red bell pepper
- Salt and pepper to taste

For serving:

- 8 small tortillas corn or flour, gluten-free if needed
- Shredded lettuce or cabbage

- Vegan sour cream optional

- Fresh lime wedges

Directions:

1. Prepare the Jackfruit Filling: Using your hands or a fork, shred the drained and rinsed jackfruit into pieces that resemble pulled pork.
2. In a large skillet, heat the olive oil over medium heat. Add the finely chopped onion and sauté for 2-3 minutes until it becomes translucent.
3. Stir in the minced garlic and cook for an additional 1-2 minutes until the garlic is fragrant.
4. Add the shredded jackfruit to the skillet and sauté for a couple of minutes to lightly brown the edges.
5. Sprinkle the ground cumin, smoked paprika, chili powder, cayenne pepper if using, salt,

and pepper over the jackfruit. Mix well to coat the jackfruit with the flavorful spices.

6. Pour the vegetable broth into the skillet to help soften the jackfruit and infuse it with the spices. Let it simmer for about 5 minutes.
7. Add the vegan barbecue sauce and lime juice to the skillet. Continue cooking the jackfruit for another 5-7 minutes until it absorbs the flavors and becomes tender.
8. Adjust the seasoning with more salt, pepper, or spices if needed. Remove the skillet from heat and set the jackfruit filling aside.
9. Prepare the Mango Salsa: In a mixing bowl, combine the diced mango, red bell pepper, red onion, jalapeño if using, and chopped cilantro.
10. Drizzle the lime juice over the salsa and toss everything together. Season with salt and pepper to taste. Set the mango salsa aside.

11. Warm the tortillas in a dry skillet or microwave.

Assembly:

12. Place a spoonful of the flavorful Vegan Jackfruit Filling on each tortilla.
13. Top the jackfruit with shredded lettuce or cabbage for added crunch and freshness.
14. Add a generous scoop of the vibrant Mango Salsa over the tacos, providing a burst of sweetness and tanginess.
15. For extra creaminess, you can drizzle some vegan sour cream over the tacos, if desired.
16. Squeeze fresh lime juice over the assembled tacos for a zesty finish.
17. Serve the mouthwatering Vegan Jackfruit Tacos with Mango Salsa on a platter or individual plates.
18. Enjoy this colorful and delicious plant-based meal as a delightful lunch or dinner option, perfect for gatherings, taco nights, or

whenever you're in the mood for a tropical twist on classic tacos!

Citrus Miso Ramen With Grilled Tempeh

Ingredients:

- 1/4 cup white miso paste
- 2 tbsp orange juice
- 1 tbsp soy sauce
- 1 tbsp sesame oil
- 1 tbsp rice vinegar
- 1 cup baby bok choy, halved
- 7 oz ramen noodles
- 1 pack tempeh, sliced
- 4 cups vegetable broth
- 1 orange, segmented

Directions:

1. Cook ramen noodles according to package Directions::. Drain and set aside.
2. Grill tempeh slices until golden brown.
3. In a pot, whisk together vegetable broth, miso paste, orange juice, soy sauce, sesame oil, and rice vinegar. Simmer for 15 minutes.
4. Add baby bok choy to the broth. Cook until tender.
5. Divide noodles into bowls, ladle hot broth over them, and top with grilled tempeh and orange segments.

Miso Ramen With Kimchi And Enoki Mushrooms

Ingredients:

- 4 cups vegetable broth
- 1/3 cup white miso paste
- 2 tbsp soy sauce
- 1 tbsp sesame oil
- 1 tbsp rice vinegar
- 9 oz ramen noodles
- 1 cup kimchi
- 1 cup enoki mushrooms, separated
- 3 green onions, sliced

Directions:

1. Cook ramen noodles according to package Directions:::. Drain and set aside.

2. In a pot, whisk together vegetable broth, miso paste, soy sauce, sesame oil, and rice vinegar. Simmer for 15 minutes.
3. Add kimchi and enoki mushrooms to the broth. Cook until mushrooms are tender.
4. Divide noodles into bowls, ladle hot broth over them, and top with sliced green onions.

Pumpkin Miso Ramen With Sage-Infused Broth

Ingredients:

- 4 cups vegetable broth
- 1/4 cup white miso paste
- 2 tbsp soy sauce
- 1 tbsp sesame oil
- 1 tbsp fresh sage leaves
- 1 tbsp maple syrup
- 1 cup kale, chopped
- 10 oz ramen noodles
- 1 cup pumpkin puree
- Toasted pumpkin seeds for garnish

Directions:

1. Cook ramen noodles according to package Directions:::. Drain and set aside.
2. In a pot, whisk together vegetable broth, miso paste, soy sauce, sesame oil, pumpkin puree, sage leaves, and maple syrup. Simmer for 20 minutes.
3. Add chopped kale to the broth. Cook until kale is wilted.
4. Divide noodles into bowls, ladle hot broth over them, and top with toasted pumpkin seeds.

Baked Cauliflower Wings

Ingredients:

- 3/4 cup milk dairy or non-dairy
- 1 teaspoon garlic powder
- 1 teaspoon paprika
- Salt and pepper to taste
- 1 head cauliflower, cut into florets
- 3/4 cup flour all-purpose or chickpea flour for a gluten-free alternative
- Buffalo sauce or BBQ sauce for coating

Directions:
1. In a bowl, mix the flour, milk, garlic powder, paprika, salt, and pepper to produce a batter.
2. Dip each cauliflower floret into the batter, covering it fully, and lay them on the prepared baking sheet.

3. Bake for 20-25 minutes or until brown and crispy.
4. Toss the cooked cauliflower wings with your choice of buffalo sauce or BBQ sauce for a savory variation.

Mini Veggie Pizzas

Ingredients:

- Shredded mozzarella cheese or dairy-free substitute
- Assorted veggies bell peppers, cherry tomatoes, mushrooms, onions, spinach
- English muffins or small pizza crusts
- Pizza sauce or marinara sauce
- Optional: Pepperoni pieces, olives, fresh basil leaves

Directions:
1. Preheat oven to 375°F 190°C.
2. Split the English muffins in half or put the tiny pizza crusts on a baking sheet.
3. Spread pizza sauce or marinara sauce equally over the surface.

4. Sprinkle shredded mozzarella cheese over the sauce.
5. Top with mixed veggies and any extra toppings of your choosing.
6. Bake for 10-12 minutes or until the cheese melts and the crust is golden brown.
7. Serve these Mini Veggie Pizzas as a crowd-pleasing starter.

Lentil And Veggie Patties

Ingredients:

- 1/2 cup bread crumbs or rolled oats

- 1 egg or flax egg for a vegan alternative

- 1 teaspoon garlic powder

- Salt and pepper to taste

- 1 cup cooked lentils green or brown

- 1 cup mixed finely chopped veggies carrots, bell peppers, onions, spinach

- Olive oil for frying

Directions:

1. In a mixing bowl, add cooked lentils, chopped veggies, bread crumbs or rolled oats, egg, garlic powder, salt, and pepper. Mix thoroughly.

2. Form the mixture into patties using your hands.
3. Heat olive oil in a pan over medium heat.
4. Cook the lentil and vegetable patties for 3-4 minutes on each side or until golden brown and cooked through.
5. Serve these tasty Lentil and Veggie Patties as a pleasant snack or dinner complement.

Black Bean Lentil Salad

Ingredients:

- 2/3 cup Cilantro
- 1 cup Green Lentils
- 2 Roma Tomatoes, diced
- 15 oz. Black Beans
- 1 Red Bell Pepper, diced
- 1 Cucumber, diced
- ½ of 1 Red Onion, small & diced

For dressing:

- 1 tsp. Cumin
- 1 tsp. Dijon Mustard
- 2 Garlic cloves
- ½ tsp. Oregano

- Juice of 1 Lime

- 1/8 tsp. Salt

- 2 tbsp. Olive Oil

Directions:

1. To begin with, cook the lentils in a large pan over a medium heat following the manufacturer's Directions::. Tip: The lentils should be cooked to firm but not mushy.
2. In the meantime, mix all the Ingredients: needed to make the dressing in a small bowl until combined well.
3. After that, combine the beans with the bell pepper, red onion cilantro, and cucumber. Spoon on the dressing.
4. Toss well and serve immediately.

www.ingramcontent.com/pod-product-compliance
Lightning Source LLC
LaVergne TN
LVHW010226070526
838199LV00062B/4740